The Power of the Wind

Mary Beth Crum

Contents

Rigby®

The Wind and You

Have you ever felt the wind on your face? It can feel warm on a hot day and cool on a cold day. Wind can also do things. It moves boats on the water. It lifts kites in the air. It even dries clothes. Sometimes we need the wind!

children flying kites

clothing drying in the wind

The Wind and Plants

The wind helps living things, too. It blows plant seeds on the ground so new plants can grow.

seeds in the wind

4

The wind helps a tumbleweed spread its seeds in a different way. The whole plant breaks off and rolls in the wind. Thousands of seeds drop as it moves.

The Wind and Animals

How does the wind help animals? If the wind is blowing in the same direction that the birds are flying, the birds will fly faster. Some birds can ride the wind. They find warm air and ride on it for miles without flapping their wings.

a bird riding the wind

6

spiders riding the wind

Small spiders can ride the wind, too. The spider sprays a string of silk in the air. The wind blows the string away, and the spider goes for a ride.

7

The Wind and Weather

Sometimes wind is dangerous. It can cause storms that may hurt people and animals.

Tornadoes happen when a lot of warm air runs into a lot of cooler air. The air spins very fast. A tornado can carry away parked cars and trains!

a tornado

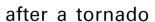

after a tornado

Hurricanes are windy storms that start over the ocean. They spin, and they make large waves in the water. Wind in a hurricane moves very fast. A hurricane can blow large objects and move them long distances.

a hurricane

Have you seen a cloud of dust that is bigger than a house? When dirt on a farm is very dry, it is like dust. Strong wind can blow huge clouds of this dust for thousands of miles. This is a dust storm. In a dust storm, dirt can blow into your eyes and mouth.

a dust storm

The Wind and Energy

People use the power of wind for energy. Some boats and ships have sails. The wind blows on the sails and the ships move. The wind is very important to the people on these ships.

Tall fans that make energy from the wind are called windmills. The wind turns the windmill, which is hooked up to a machine. The machine then makes electricity.

Problems with Wind Power

There can be problems with using wind power, too. Some people think that windmills are noisy. It can be dangerous for birds if they fly near the windmill. Also, there is not always enough wind to make the windmill move.

a windmill

The Future of Wind Power

More and more, people will use the wind for energy. One day the light in your classroom may use wind power!

Index